C000319077

# Victorian Cottage Gardens

Text: David Squire

Editor: Laura Potts

Design: Alison Jewell and Philip Clucas

Photographs: Fine Art Photographs and
Library Ltd.

Production Director: Gerald Hughes

Production: Ruth Arthur, Sally Connolly,
Neil Randles

Acknowledgements to the legatees of Mrs G. Ashburner
for Picking Lavender by William F. Ashburner, p.55.
While every effort has been made to contact copyright
holders, the publisher would welcome information on
any oversight which may have occurred.

CLB 4242
Published in 1994 by Bramley Books for
Selecta Books Ltd, Devizes
© 1994 Bramley Books
All rights reserved.
Printed and bound in Italy.
ISBN 1 85833 181 1

# Victorian Cottage Gardens

A Wayside Cottage on the Bredon
*George H. Hughes (fl.1813–1858), private collection.*

SELECT
EDITIONS

The Cottage Guard
*Arthur Claude Strachan (1865-1954), Philip Gale.*

# Contents

*I knew by the smoke that so gracefully curled*
*Above the green elms, that a cottage was*
    *near,*
*And I said, 'If there's peace to be found in*
  *the world,*
*A heart that was humble might hope for it*
  *here.'*
Thomas Moore ( 1779-1852)

# Introduction

E ven the name cottage garden is enough to conjure an image of a garden filled with a casual medley of flowers, shrubs, vegetables, culinary and medicinal herbs and fruit trees, with a meandering path leading to a front door drenched in colourful and highly scented climbers. It evokes thoughts of entire gardens allotted to plants, from boundary to front door, without the decadent luxury of a lawn, and enclosed by a hedge or low wall.

The art of a cottage garden is not to regiment nature, only to curb its excesses, to grow food and herbal plants and to unify and brighten the area with flowers.

### Diverse Views

The industrial revolution was to change dramatically the landscape of nineteenth-century Britain. Traditionalists and moralists increasingly questioned and compared town cottages with ones in rural areas, which they idolised for the socially unifying qualities performed by 'hollyhocks, beehives and honeysuckle'. Yet for many the idealistic cottage garden portrayed in literature and art was only a recent innovation.

Feeding Doves, Near Frome, Somerset
*Arthur Claude Strachan (1865-1954), Galerie George.*

An English Cottage Garden *James Matthews, City Wall Gallery.*

Certainly, it was likely that the picturesque cottage garden was more to be seen around small farmhouses than those of labourers, for whom food production, rather than aesthetics of flowers, must have been the priority.

## Revivalist Thoughts

A 'rose is a rose' and whatever the terminology the idealistic cottage garden became increasingly fashionable and desirable during the eighteenth century. Despite the increasing range of plants introduced from warm climates in the first half of the nineteenth century, the majority of cottage gardens continued with their traditional flowering plants, mainly with an herbaceous nature.

The gardener William Robinson extolled informality and mixtures of plants and towards the end of the nineteenth century erroneously claimed that by the 1880s herbaceous plants had all but disappeared. He further suggested that their later popularity was due to him and his rediscovery of them in cottage gardens. It was true that cottage gardens were repositories for herbaceous plants, but so too were large estates, and nurseries never ceased growing them. Although Robinson did proclaim the virtues of informality and mixed planting, others voiced similar thoughts before and during his apostolic stance.

The idealistic cottage garden, therefore, continued through the nineteenth century, although the writings of reformers during the early to middle part of the century advocated emphasis on vegetables and fruits. In part this was due to the efforts of the Young England movement, which campaigned in the 1830s and 1840s for the provision of allotments.

Where cottagers were tenants of local landowners they were frequently made to concentrate on floral displays, such as roses around doors. Herbaceous perennials were popular as they were easily and inexpensively increased and did not need coddling. This is not to say that slowly, from about the middle of the nineteenth century, tender plants such as calceolarias, pelargoniums and verbenas were not introduced. They were planted, though in reserved numbers, and their use was totally dissimilar from that of the half-hardy annuals, which were planted in disciplined patterns in borders, a style that was fashionable in the late nineteenth century.

## The Artistic Eye

Painters and engravers throughout the centuries captured the botanical images of plants, perhaps none better known than by the works of the Belgian Pierre-Joseph Redoute who during the early years of the nineteenth century was commissioned by Josephine Bonaparte to paint plants in her garden at Malmaison, near Paris. Redoute, however, was a botanical artist and it was left to others to capture entire gardens on canvas. Many artists during the eighteenth century were enthused by the rustic and lax nature of cottage gardens. It was an interpretation of life and the changing patterns of the country. The English landscape painter John Constable during the late eighteenth and early nineteenth centuries imparted realism to his studies and included broken fences, damaged and unappealing cottages and dirty cottagers. Later painters were to view cottage gardens with a sunnier disposition. Whereas reality might be a dingy cottage and few flowers, the genie within each painter's eye saw a different scene that has, through subsequent years, produced carefree and smiling cottagers and gardens abounding in colour.
Not all painters, however, glossed over the hardships of cottage life. Helen Allingham painted gardens showing them as they were, bringing to her work the same realistic approach which characterised the poems of her husband, William Allingham.

Lambing Time
*Basil Bradley (1842-1904), Bourne Gallery.*

## From Flowers to Food

Cottage gardens were repositories of many types of plants, from those that were solely decorative to ones that had culinary and medicinal uses. Vegetables and fruits were also essential. The multi-purpose nature of the cottage garden is reflected in the sections into which the book is divided.

The Floral Garden parades cottage garden plants, such as hollyhocks, golden rod and larkspur that for centuries introduced a lax, casual aura to gardens and will forever be associated with the traditional cottage garden.

The Scented Garden celebrates plants whose sweet scents have characterised cottage gardens for centuries. Scented gardens never cease to arouse interest; some are at their best during the day while others drench windows with rich bouquets and fragrances throughout evening and at night. And no cottage garden would be complete without a scented bower, nestling in a warm, wind-sheltered corner and smothered in scented climbing plants steeped in romanticism.

The Herb Garden features culinary and medicinal herbs, such as sage, thyme, parsley, mint and marjoram, which are continuing legacies from monastic gardens. Medicinal plants were also widely known and these too are traditional parts of herb borders, later essential to cottagers and frequently grown near to entrances.

The Fruits of the Garden covers any food plant, including autumn and summer fruits and vegetables. Apples, pears, cherries, damsons and plums have long been grown in England; the Romans catalogued several varieties of apples, while the damson, a close relative of plums, takes its name from Damascus and has been grown since before the Christian era. Its original name was damascene. Many vegetables have long been established in gardens, perhaps none better known than leeks and cabbage that were grown by the Romans. The potato, introduced much later from South America, soon became a staple part of diets, together with carrots, parsnips, runner beans, onions and cauliflowers.

At the Cottage Gate
*Helen Allingham (1848-1926), Harper Fine Paintings.*

Yew Arches
*George Samuel Elgood (1851-1943), Gavin Graham Gallery.*

# The Floral Garden

In the Garden
*Joseph Kirkpatrick (fl.1898-1928),*
*City Wall Gallery*

*A detail from*
A Cottage Garden in
Devon.

## THE PRIMROSE

*Dost ask me, why I send thee here,*
*This firstling of the infant year –*
*This lovely native of the vale,*
*That hangs so pensive and so pale?*

*Look on its bending stalk, so weak*
*That, each way yielding, doth not break,*
*And see how aptly it reveals*
*The doubts and fears a lover feels.*

*Look on its leaves of yellow hue*
*Bepearl'd thus with morning dew,*
*And these will whisper in thine ears*
*'The sweets of love are wash'd with tears.*

Robert Burns (1759-96)

# *Primroses*

Almost all plants, at one time, have been claimed to have herbal powers and the primrose is no exception, for it was believed that the whole plant had sedative qualities. Indeed, an infusion of the flowers has been recommended to remove nervous hysteria and tension. The sixteenth-century barber-surgeon John Gerard noted that primrose tea was famous for curing the 'phrensie'.

*... the primrose path of dalliance treads.*
(William Shakespeare - Hamlet)

Spring Flowers
*Emma Cooper (b. 1837), Bourne Gallery.*

A Cottage Garden in Devon
*Fritz Althaus (fl.1881-1914), Hampshire Gallery.*

## THE SPRING

*Now that the winter's gone, the earth hath lost*
*Her snow-white robes; and now no more the frost*
*Candies the grasse, or castes an ycie creame*
*Upon the silver Lake or Chrystall streame:*
*But the warme Sunne thawes the benummed earth,*
*And makes it tender; gives a sacred birth*
*To the dead Swallow; wakes in hollow tree*
*The drowzie Cuckow and the Humble-Bee.*
*Now doe a quire of chirping minstrels bring,*
*In tryumph to the world, the youthfull Spring.*
*The vallies, hills, and woods in rich araye*
*Welcome the comming of the long'd-for May.*

Thomas Carew (?1595?1640)

Spring Blossom
*Helen Allingham (1848-1926),*
*Anthony Mitchell Paintings.*

# *Blossom*

Certainly, few sights in an orchard are as captivating as the pink and white blossom of apples in May. Through the centuries poets have sought to praise apple blossom in verse, celebrating its beauty and its transient, seasonal nature. Shakespeare wrote 'Rough winds do shake the darling buds of May'. Apple blossoms occur in trusses usually formed by a central blossom and surrounded by six others. Though some varieties do show a variation in their flowers, in the degrees of colour, size and shape, these differences are only slight.

In Victorian England May Birchers went on their rounds fixing branches of blossom and other plants to the doors of houses, reflecting their thoughts about the occupants, both good and bad. For example, if a branch of hawthorn was nailed to the door your neighbours thought well of you, while if branches of other thorn trees were found, you could be sure that you had attracted their scorn. Rhyming slang was central to understanding the meanings of the branches. The rowan or wicken, which rhymes with chicken, was a sign of affection, while holly signified folly and briar implied a liar.

Blossom
*Percival Moore (fl.c. 1915), private collection.*

A Cottage Garden
*John Horner (fl.1881-1891), Cooper Fine Arts.*

Gathering Flowers
*Florence Agnes Mackay (fl.c. 1896) Walker Galleries.*

## SPRING FLOWERS

*Along the blushing borders bright with dew*
*And in yon mingled wilderness of flowers,*
*Fair-handed Spring unbosoms every grace:*
*Throws out the snow-drop and the crocus first;*
*The daisy, primrose, violet darkly blue,*
*And polyanthus of unnumbered dyes;*
*The yellow wall-flower, stained with iron brown,*
*And lavish stock that scents the garden round:*
*From the soft wing of vernal breezes shed,*
*Anemonies; auriculas, enriched*
*With shining meal o'er all their velvet leaves;*
*And full ranunculas, of glowing red.*
*Then comes the tulip-race, where Beauty plays*
*Her idle freaks: from family diffused*
*To family, as flies the father-dust,*
*The varied colours run; and while they break*
*On the charmed eye, the exulting florist marks,*
*With secret pride, the wonders of his hand.*
*No gradual bloom is wanting; from the bud*
*First-born of Spring, to Summer's musky tribes:*
*Nor hyacinths, deep-purpled; nor jonquils,*
*Of potent fragrance; nor narcissus fair,*
*As o'er the fabled fountain hanging still;*
*Nor broad carnations, nor gay-spotted pinks;*
*Nor, showered from every bush, the damask-rose:*
*Infinite numbers, delicacies, smells,*
*With hues on hues expression cannot paint,*
*The breath of Nature, and her endless bloom.*

James Thomson (1700-48)

# Daisies

Daisies have peppered gardens for hundreds of years, in lawns, between paving stones and as border edgings. Throughout the centuries many gardeners have regularly purified lawns by grubbing them out, but to many eyes they have such a natural and bright look that they are left undisturbed. Indeed, there is an old proverb that says 'When you can put a foot on seven daisies, summer is come'. Other sayings, perhaps not so optimistic about the sunny season, mention only five daisies! Our Anglo-Saxon ancestors knew this plant as daezeseze, referring to its flowers which close at night and open each morning. Later, it was better known to lovers as measure of love; petals were pulled off to the chant 'he loves me, he loves me not'. While in Scotland it was commonly known as bairnwort and widely used by children to form chains of flowers.

*from* IS LIFE WORTH LIVING?

*While children in the woodlands yet*
*Adorn their little laps*
*With ladysmock and violets,*
*And daisy chain their caps;*

Alfred Austin (1835-1913)

*A detail from*
April in the Meadows

The Daisy Chain
*Florence Fitzgerald (d.1927), Christopher Cole Paintings.*

22

# YOUTH

*Sweet empty sky of June without a stain*
*  Faint, gray-blue dewy mists on far-off hills,*
*Warm, yellow sunlight flooding mead and plain,*
*  That each dark copse and hollow overfills;*
*  The rippling laugh of unseen, fain-fed rills,*
*Weeds delicate-flowered, white and pink and gold,*
*A murmur and singing manifold.*

*The gray, austere old earth renews her youth*
*  With dew-lines, sunshine, gossamer and haze.*
*How still she lies and dreams, and veils the truth,*
*  While all is fresh as in the early days!*
*  What simple things be these the soul to raise*
*To bounding joy, and make young pulses beat,*
*With nameless pleasure finding life so sweet.*

*On such a golden morning forth there floats,*
*  Between the soft earth and the softer sky,*
*In the warm air adust with glistening motes,*
*  The mystic winged and flickering butterfly,*
*  A human soul, that hovers giddily*
*Among the gardens of earth's paradise,*
*Nor dreams of fairer fields or loftier skies.*

Emma Lazarus (1849-87)
From 'Epochs', a series of sixteen poems

April in the Meadows
*William Bartlett (1858-1932),*
*Bourne Gallery.*

A Cheshire Cottage
*Arthur Claude Strachan (1865-1954), Marian and John Alway.*

*A detail from*
A Cheshire Cottage.

The Herbacious Border
*Patrick William Adam (1854-1930), Julian Simon.*

# Tulips

Upright, soldier-like varieties of tulips were popular in cottage gardens. For the vast range of tulip varieties we are, in part, indebted to the Dutch. The mania for tulip bulbs reached its height in the early seventeenth century when the bulbs were so highly prized that a single bulb was sold for £400. The bulbs were so valuable that in one case a dowry was received in the form of a rare bulb and in another a miller exchanged his mill for a bulb. This bulb bonanza ended in 1637, when a law was enacted compelling transactions to be completed like those of any other business, bringing to an end the speculation that had fuelled the mania. Once the price of the bulbs stabilised and came within the reach of the ordinary income, tulips came to be more widely grown, and by the nineteenth century had become one of the prerequisites of the traditional cottage garden.

# Forget-me-nots

Few spring and early summer borders would be complete without the lax, blue heads of forget-me-nots forming a backdrop for tulips. Stories about how the forget-me-not got its name abound. A German legend tells of a knight who saw the pretty flowers growing by a stream and began to collect them for his lady. As he did so, he fell in and was swept away by the water, calling to his love as he went 'Forget me not'. Another tale tells how a little blue plant kept forgetting its name and how God, tired by the endless questions, said that it should be called forget-me-not. The gentle charms of the forget-me-not have been celebrated in literature and during the early 1800s, the poet Samuel Taylor Coleridge wrote:

*The blue and bright-eye flowerer of the brook,*
*Hope's gentle gem - the sweet forget-me-not.*

# Flag Iris

North End House, Rottingdean
*Thomas Matthews Rooke (1842-1942),*
*private collection.*

Known as flag iris, purple flag and London flag, *Iris germanica* is probably one of the oldest cultivated irises and was grown in Europe as early as the thirteenth century. Orris Root, widely used in perfumery, is derived from *I. g. florentina* and for centuries was used in the preparation of toiletries. The roots were washed, cut into small slices, threaded and allowed to dry. The fragrance usually did not appear until after two years of drying. Apart from being used in toiletries, beads of it were put in rosaries, were burned to scent rooms, and were given to teething infants. It was also used to sweeten breath and men servants chewed it to remove the odour of tobacco and garlic.

*A detail from*
North End House

# Lilies

The perfection and desirability of lilies has been recognised for several thousand years and generated many sayings, perhaps none more meaningful than an old Chinese proverb:

*When you have only two pennies left in the world,*
*buy a loaf of bread with one and a lily with the other.*

Throughout the centuries, lilies have stood regally among other plants, many with dominantly white flowers that have encouraged the use of slang references, especially during the early 1800s and throughout the Victorian era: a Lily Shallow was a white driving hat, a Lily Benjamin a white greatcoat, and Lily-white Groat for a shilling. While from about 1700 to 1830 a Lily-white was a chimney-sweep.

*A detail from*
Young Girl by a Garden Gate

Young Girl by a Garden Gate
*Mildred Butler (1858-1941), Hampshire Gallery.*

Feeding a Pony in a Surrey Garden
*Edward Killingworth Johnson (1825-1923), private collection.*

Pansies and Primroses,
*Vincent Clare (c.1855-1930),*
*Beaton Brown Fine Paintings.*

*A detail from*
Feeding a Pony in a Surrey Garden

# Poppies

Before the introduction of mechanised harvesting and weed killers, many plants were notoriously troublesome in fields at harvest time. So pernicious was the field poppy (*Papaver rhoeas*) that it was known as headache, canker and redweed. The seeds are carried by the wind and poppies from surrounding fields often quickly laid territorial claim to cottage gardens. The field poppy has an unforgettable image when seen en masse. The notorious opium poppy (*P. somniferum*), from Greece and the Orient, is perhaps the oldest poppy in cultivation and was probably introduced into England by the Romans. By the middle of the eighteenth century, many forms existed, with highly descriptive names such as curled poppy, fringed poppy and feathered poppy.

# Violas

Grassy banks carpeted in violas, thyme and oxlips are an enchanting and idyllic Shakespearean legacy, enthusiastically encouraged on many short-grassed, sun-soaked knolls. The viola or heart's ease (*Viola tricolor*) known to the Elizabethans is not unlike today's large-flowered pansies. No sloth when accumulating common names, the viola is known by sixty or more, including love-in-idleness, kiss-her-in-the-buttery and cuddle-me. In the sixteenth century, Edmund Spenser referred to 'The pretty pawnce' and William Shakespeare to 'Pansies, that's for thoughts', both derived from the French *pensée*. However, during the eighteenth century, Samuel Johnson suggested that the name pansy derived from panacea, on account of it being a remedy for the French pox.

# Nasturtiums

The first nasturtium to arrive in England was not the one widely-grown in cottage gardens during nineteenth century and today. Although similar to the now popular *Tropaeolum majus*, the first nasturtiums to appear were the now more-or-less-unknown *T. minus*, familiar to the late sixteenth- and early seventeenth-century gardener John Gerard as yellow larkes spurr and frequently recommended for inclusion in delicate tussiemussies or nosegays. The nasturtium of later cottage gardens did not arrive until 1684, with the dwarf or Tom Thumb varieties appearing in Victorian times. The popular seed-raised Gleam strain, which was widely acclaimed in Britain in the early 1930s, originated in a cottage garden in California. As well as brightening cottage gardens, the leaves and flowers of nasturtiums were frequently added to salads.

*A detail from*
Among the Nasturtiums.

Tending the Nasturtiums.
*A. Templeuve, private collection.*

Among the Nasturtiums
*Hector Caffieri (1847-1932), Cooper Fine Art, London.*

At Allerford, Somerset
*Arthur Claude Strachan (1865-1954), Burlington Paintings.*

# *Hollyhocks*

It is thought that Crusaders returning from the Holy Land during the eleventh, twelfth and thirteenth centuries introduced hollyhocks (*Alcea rosea* but earlier *Althaea rosea*) to Europe and Britain. Initially the plants were known as holy-hock, from the Anglo-Saxon word *hoc*, meaning mallow. Later they came to be called holyhoke and holyoke. Huguenots, who fled their native France in the late 1600s, knew these spire-like plants as outlandish rose and rose ultramarina. Prior to Queen Victoria's coronation in 1837 – encouraged by botanical confirmation that cotton is produced from a related plant – attempts were made to grow hollyhocks to provide fibres for cloth making. This was unsuccessful, but hollyhock flowers have yielded a blue dye, said to equal the best indigo.

## A Garden Song

*Here, in this sequestered close,*
*Bloom the hyacinth and rose;*
*Here beside the modest stock*
*Flaunts the flaring hollyhock;*
*Here, without a pang, one sees*
*Ranks, conditions, and degrees.*

*All the seasons run their race*
*In this quiet resting place;*
*Peach, and apricot, and fig*
*Here will ripen, and grow big*
*Here is store and overplus,–*
*More had not Alcinous!*

*Here, in alleys cool and green,*
*Far ahead the thrush is seen;*
*Here along the southern wall*
*Keeps the bee his festival;*
*All is quiet else-afar*
*Sounds of toil and turmoil are.*

*Here be shadows large and long;*
*Here be spaces meet for song;*
*Grant, O garden-god, that I,*
*Now that mood and moment please,–*
*Find the fair Pierides!*

Henry Austin Dobson (1840-1921)

By the Cottage Door
*Arthur Claude Strachan (1865-1954),*
*Galerie George.*

# Clematis

Even the name clematis conjures thoughts of romantic, leafy canopies. The British native, traveller's joy (*Clematis vitalba*) is a familiar climber of hedgerows, with faintly-scented, greenish-white flowers followed by silky seed-heads that last throughout winter and are especially attractive when covered by frost. Its other name, old man's beard, wonderfully describes the seed-heads. As well as decorating hedgerows and gardens, young shoots were eaten as a vegetable. The roots and stems when boiled in water and then put in sweet oil were used as a cure for 'itch', a contagious disease caused by itch mites. While the sweetly-scented Virgin's bower (*C. flagella*), native to southern Europe, has sweetly-scented white flowers from mid-summer to autumn. Another clematis associated with bowers is *C. recta*, an herbaceous species from Europe and Asia. Like traveller's joy, it has medicinal qualities, which must have been potent because antidotes for excessive doses were suggested; one is Bryan to appease the toothache caused by clematis.

*A detail from*
Cottages on the River.

Through the Garden Door
*George Sheridan Knowles ,*
*Gavin Graham Gallery*

Cottages on the River
*Arthur Claude Strachan (1865-1954), Mr Fulda.*

Talking to the Ducks
*Arthur Claude Strachan (1865-1954),*
*private collection.*

At the Village Ford
*Arthur Claude Strachan (1865-1954),*
*Anthony Mitchell Fine Paintings.*

# Foxgloves

Foxgloves have occasionally been thought to represent the darker side of life as they grow in shaded places. Druids were especially fond of their flowers, which appeared at the time of mid-summer sacrifices and have wide medicinal properties. The plant gained the Anglo-Saxon name foxes-gleow because it resembled a gleow, a musical instrument formed of an arch bearing a ring of bells in graduated sizes. Other names include witches' gloves, fairy's glove, dead men's bells, fairy thimbles, virgin's glove, floppydock and flowster-docken.

*Detail of* At the Village Ford.

Outside the Cottage
*Arthur Claude Strachan (1865-1954), private colledtion.*

A Picturesque Cottage Garden
*Arthur Claude Strachan (1865-1954),*
*Anthony Mitchell Paintings.*

*A detail from*
A Picturesque Cottage Garden.

# Antirrhinum

These colourful cottage garden plants, sometimes called lion's mouth and calves' snout, are best known to children as snapdragons because their dragon-like flowers can be manipulated to open and close. Snapdragons (*Antirrhinum majus*), originally from southern Europe, spread to Britain and soon became naturalised. In gardens it is usually grown as a half-hardy perennial and raised in gentle warm weather in spring. When left to its natural inclinations, however, it soon finds a warm, sheltered corner and resumes a perennial nature. A maestro at clinging to life between joints in old walls, it can turn a barren feature into one smothered in colour and as such has long been a favourite in cottage gardens.

# Calendula

Marigolds (*Calendula officinalis*) exude a cottage-garden presence, radiating brightness and a relaxed nature. They especially reveal a natural life-style when their petals fall. It is thought that this southern European plant arrived in Britain in the thirteenth century. Known to early English writers as ruddes and summer's bride, the marigold soon established itself as a garden delight and herbal wonder. It was said that looking at marigolds each day gave protection from fevers. William Shakespeare wrote that the marigold goes to bed with the sun and later the imprisoned king, Charles I, sadly observed:

*The Marigold observes the Sun*
*More than my Subjects me have done ...*

At the Garden Gate
*George F. Nicholls (fl.1885-1937), private collection.*

## EUTOPIA

*There is a garden where lilies*
  *And roses are side by side;*
*And all day between them in silence*
  *The silken butterflies glide.*

*I may not enter the garden,*
  *Though I know the road thereto;*
*And morn by morn to the gateway*
  *I see the children go.*

*They bring back light on their faces;*
  *But they cannot bring back to me*
*What the lilies say to the roses*
  *Or the songs of the butterflies be.*

Francis Turner Palgrave (1824–1897)

*A detail from*
A Mother's Welcome.

A Mother's Welcome
*Henry John King (1855-1924), Haynes Fine Art.*

Out of School
*Myles Birket Foster (1825-1899), Polak Gallery.*

Pretty Cottages on a Summer's Day
*Arthur Claude Strachan (1865-1954), City Wall Gallery.*

## *from* THE GARDEN IN SEPTEMBER

*Now thin mists temper the slow-ripening beams*
*Of the September sun: his golden gleams*
*On gaudy flowers shine, that prank the rows*
*Of high-grown hollyhocks, and all tall shows*
*That Autumn flaunteth in his bushy bowers;*
*Where tomtits, hanging from the drooping heads*
*Of giant sunflowers, peck the nutty seeds;*
*And in the feathery aster bees on wing*
*Seize and set free the honied flowers,*
*Till thousand stars leap with their visiting:*
*While ever across the path mazily flit,*
*Unpiloted in the sun,*
*The dreamy butterflies*
*With dazzling colours powdered and soft glooms,*
*White, black and crimson stripes, and peacock eyes,*
*Or on chance flowers sit,*
*With idle effort plundering one by one*
*The nectaries of deepest-throated blooms.*

Robert Bridges (1844-1930)

*Giving a helping hand, detail from*
Out of School.

In the Rose Garden
*Thomas James Lloyd (1849-1910), Bourne Gallery.*

# The Scented Garden

Still Life with Roses
*C.F. Hurten (1818-1897), Caelt Gallery.*

A Cottage Garden
*James Matthews (fl.c. 1900),*
*Church Street Gallery.*

# Apple Blossom

Few country sights are as pleasing and so full of promise for a bountiful harvest as apple trees laden with lightly-fragrant blossom. The first century Roman statesman and writer Pliny tells of several varieties and, undoubtedly, many of these were introduced into Britain by the Romans. By the end of the thirteenth century, the Pearmain apple, which remained the main dessert apple for hundreds of years, was established. Another famous type of apple, the Costard, was widely recorded in the thirteenth century and was superb in pies. By the seventeenth century, the Costard apple had all but disappeared and today the name is only remembered in the word 'costermonger', which originally meant a purveyor of Costard apples but in Victorian times came to mean a hawker of fruit, vegetables and fish.

Apple Blossom and Primulas,
*Oliver Clare (fl.1853-1927),*
*Anthony Mitchell Fine Paintings.*

## O Lady, Leave Thy Silken Thread

*O Lady, leave thy silken thread*
  *And flowery tapestry,*
*There's living roses on the bush,*
  *And blossoms on the tree;*
*Stoop where thou wilt, thy careless hand*
  *Some random bud will meet;*
*Thou canst not tread, but thou wilt find*
  *The daisy at thy feet.*

*'Tis like the birthday of the world,*
  *When earth was born in bloom;*
*The light is made of many dyes,*
  *The air is all perfume;*
*There's crimson buds, and white and blue—*
  *The very rainbow showers*
*Have turned to blossoms where they fell,*
  *And sown the earth with flowers.*

*There's fairy tulips in the East,*
  *The garden of the sun;*
*The very streams reflect the hues,*
  *And blossom as they run:*
*While morn opes like a crimson rose,*
  *Still wet with pearly showers;*
*Then Lady, leave the silken thread*
  *Thou twinest into flowers.*

Thomas Hood (1799-1845)

Springtime
*David Woodlock (1842-1929), Mr Fulda.*

Daisies by the Cottage Door
*Thomas Mackay (fl.1893-1916), Philip Gale.*

## *from* THE EXCURSION

*Her cottage, then a cheerful object, wore*
*Its customary look, – only, it seemed,*
*The honeysuckle, crowding round the porch,*
*Hung down in heavier tufts; and that bright weed,*
*The yellow stone-crop, suffered to take root*
*Along the window's edge, profusely grew*
*Blinding the lower panes. I turned aside*
*And strolled into her garden. It appeared*
*To lag behind the season, and had lost*
*Its pride of neatness. Daisy-flowers and thrift*
*Had broken their trim border-lines, and straggled*
*O'er paths they used to deck:*

William Wordsworth (1770-1850)

*Detail from*
Daisies by the Cottage Door.

*Detail from*
In the Garden

*from* PROPOSALS FOR
BUILDING A COTTAGE

*A little garden, not too fine,*
*Inclose with painted pales;*
*And woodbines, round the cot to twine,*
*Pin to the wall with nails.*

*Let hazels grow, and spindling sedge,*
*Bend bowering over-head;*
*Dig old man's beard from woodland hedge,*
*To twine a summer shade.*

John Clare (1793-1864)

# Honeysuckle

Few climbing plants have the literary fame of honeysuckle, or woodbine as it was popularly known. It was featured by William Shakespeare in *A Midsummer Night's Dream*:
*I know a bank whereon the wild thyme blows,*
*Where oxlips and the nodding violet grows*
*Quite over-canopied with luscious woodbine,*
*With sweet musk-roses, and with eglantine.*

In cottage gardens honeysuckle was frequently planted in arbours and around the entrances of cottages, where its perfume could be enjoyed by all and where its leaves would be easily accessible. Honeysuckle leaves had medicinal properties and were used in many preparations. A gargle made from honeysuckle leaves, for example, was used as a cure for sore throats, and an infusion made from its leaves was soothing for coughs.

In the Garden
*Henry John King (1855-1924), Anthony Mitchell Fine Paintings.*

A Summer's Day
*Edward Killingworth Johnson (1825-1923), Bourne Gallery.*

## *from* THE WISH

*At whose southend a harbour should be made*
*So well belov'd in summer for its shade:*
*For this the rose would do or jessamine*
*With virginbower or the sweet woodbine,*
*Each one of these would form exactly well*
*A compleat harbour both for shade or smell.*
*Here would I sit when leisure did agree*
*To view the pride of summer scenery*
*See the productions promis'd from my spade*
*While blest with liberty and cooling shade.*

John Clare (1793-1864)

Still Life, White and Pink Roses
*Rosa Appleton (fl.1880-1902),*
*private collection.*

The Rose Arch
*George Sheridan Knowles (1863-1931), Walker Gallery.*

Red Roses
*Edith Isabel Barrow (d.1930).*

# Roses

Romantic Roses
*Eugene Henri Cauchois (1850-1911),*
*Gavin Graham Gallery.*

Before Man meddled with roses, creating a near inexhaustible range of varieties, only wild types and those crossings that occurred naturally between them were available. With continued thanks to Shakespeare, the supreme publicist, most cottage gardeners since the early seventeenth century have aspired to create canopies of eglantine (*Rosa rubiginosa*), or sweetbriar as it was also known. The bright-pink, single flowers appear amid sweetly-fragrant leaves that are said to emit their best fragrance after a light shower and when the atmosphere is moist and fresh. These romantic flowers will be forever be associated with the cottage garden.

*Detail of* Roses

## Sonnet
Written in a country retirement

*Around my porch and lonely casement spread,*
*The myrtle never sere, and gadding vine,*
*With fragrant sweet-briar love to intertwine;*
*And in my garden's box-encircled bed*
*The pansy pied, and musk rose white and red;*
*The pink, the lily chaste, and sweet woodbine,*
*Fling odors round; thick-woven eglantine*
*Decks my trim fence; in which, by silence led,*
*The wren hath wisely built her mossy cell,*
*Shelter'd from storms, in courtly land so rife,*
*And nestles o'er her young, and warbles well.*
*'Tis here with innocence in peaceful glen*
*I pass my blameless moments far from men,*
*Nor wishing death too soon, nor asking life.*

John Codrington Bampfylde

Roses
*Harry Watson (1871-1936),*
*City Wall Gallery.*

A Worcestershire Cottage
*Arthur Claude Strachan (1865-1954), Julian Simon.*

# Lavender

Few heads do not become heady with thoughts of fragrant posies and pot pourris, sweet bags and sachets when lavender is mentioned, while the lyrical street-cry 'Who will buy my sweet lavender' echoes in many minds. The English lavender (*Lavandula angustifolia* but equally well known as *L. officinalis* and *L. vera*) brightens gardens and scents rooms. It was valued in cottage gardens, however, as much for its medicinal properties as for its scent. It was reputed to remedy barrenness in women, improve memory, prevent vertigo and cure bites from serpents and mad dogs. Lavender was certainly part of elixirs for all seasons and problems; it was even claimed to repel midges and to calm lions and tigers.

### *from* THE AFFECTIONATE SHEPHERD

*Nay more than this, I have a garden plot,*
*Wherein there wants nor herbs, nor roots, nor flowers*
*(Flowers to smell, roots to eat, herbs for the pot),*
*And dainty shelters when the welkin lours;*
*Sweet smelling beds of lilies and of roses*
*Which rosemary banks and lavender encloses.*

Richard Barnfield (1574–1627)

*Detail of*
A Worcestershire Cottage.

Picking Lavender,
*William F. Ashburner (d. 1951), Angela Hone Watercolours.*

# *Roses*

The Victorian era saw a dramatic change in roses. Species roses and their natural progeny that for centuries had featured in cottage gardens were about to be rivalled by marriages between roses from the East and West. An important development came in 1837 with the creation of a Hybrid Perpetual, a cross between a Bourbon Rose and a Portland Rose. The Hybrid Perpetual was the queen of Victorian roses and thirty years after its origination led to the development of the first Hybrid Tea rose. The Victorians took to roses enthusiastically, forming societies and holding competitions. Initially, roses were featured in general competitions, but in the late 1850s the first exhibition dedicated solely to roses was held in London. Although colour and flower form were important, the scent of the bloom was not neglected.

## YOU LOVE THE ROSES

*You love the roses – so do I. I wish*
*The sky would rain down roses, as they rain*
*From off the shaken bush. Why will it not?*
*Then all the valley would be pink and white*
*And soft to tread on. They would fall as light*
*As feathers, smelling sweet: and it would be*
*Like sleeping and yet waking, all at once.*

George Eliot (1819-80)

Leisure Moments
*Ernest Walbourn (fl.1897-1920),*
*Bourne Gallery.*

## A WHITE ROSE

*The red rose whispers of passion,*
*    And the white rose breathes of love;*
*O, the red rose is a falcon,*
*    And the white rose is a dove.*

*But I send you a cream-white rosebud*
*    With a flush on its petal tips;*
*For the love that is purest and sweetest*
*    Has a kiss of desire on the lips.*

John Boyle O'Reilly (1844-90)

Picking Posies
*William Affleck (1868-1943),*
*Bourne Gallery.*

Pink and Yellow Roses
*Jean-Baptiste Robie (1821-1910), private collection.*

# Madonna Lilies

Lilies have graced gardens for about 5,000 years and images of the Madonna lily (*Lilium candidum*) were depicted on Cretan vases. Lilies were particularly favoured by the Romans, who admired its elegant flowers and used the bulbs to help cure corns. In gardens, the white-petalled, sweetly-scented flowers with golden pollen stand out like beacons among other plants. During the seventh century, the Venerable Bede made this lily the emblem of the Resurrection of the Virgin, likening the white petals to her spotless body and the golden anthers to her soul glowing with heavenly light. William Godorus, surgeon to Queen Elizabeth I, recommended mixing the bulb's juice with barley-meal to cure dropsy.

The Garden
*Walter Crane (1845-1915),*
*private collection.*

A Still Life of Lilies and Roses
*Mary Margetts, (d.1886), Bourne Gallery.*

Contemplation
*Henry John King (1855-1924), Haynes Fine Art.*

A Wayside Cottage on the Bredon
*George H. Hughes (fl.1813-1858), private collection.*

# Malcolmia

The Virginian stock (*Malcolmia maritima*) does not, as its name suggests, originate in North America, but is a southern Mediterranean plant. Nineteenth-century garden writer Jane Webb Loudon claimed that the name could have been a corruption of Virgin's stock, because of the ease with which young girls can grow the plant. Whatever its name, its sweet scent is much to be desired and has earned the Virginian stock its place in many a cottage garden. It was frequently mixed with the taller and rather straggly night-scented stock (*Matthiola bicornis*) and sown under cottage-garden windows.

# Stocks

Stock-gilloflowers, as the species of *Matthiola* were known in Elizabethan times, gained their name from their woody stems (from the word stock meaning stick or stem) and their scent, which resembled that of the carnation or gillyflower. Today, these perfumed flowers are known simply as stocks. Most stocks are derived from our native *Matthiola incana*, but the ten-week stocks originate from the European native *M. annua*. Their scent is legend and they were often planted in borders, especially those close to doors and windows. Certainly, no cottage garden would have been complete without them.

A Cottage Garden at Sunset
*David Woodlock (1842-1929), Harper Fine Paintings.*

# Dianthus

A July Morning
*Marian Chase (1844-1905),
Gavin Graham Gallery.*

One of the earliest English common names given to *Dianthus caryophyllus* was sops-in-wine, a name which derived from the Spanish practice of adding the clove-scented flowers to wine to give it a spicy flavour. Other common names followed, among them gilofre, groomylyon and Chaucer's clove-gilofre, and then Shakespeare's gillvore. Thoughts differ about the exact origins of this name and while some believe it to be from the French word *giroflier*, meaning clove-tree, others say that its origins were Arabic. Whatever the name, these clove-scented flowers are a cottage garden delight. This species is also the main parent of border and perpetual-flowering carnations.

*Colourful border flowers, detail from*
A July Morning.

At Madehurst, Sussex
*James Matthews,*
*Burlington Paintings, London.*

# Sweet Rocket

Even the names sweet rocket and dames' violet evoke thoughts of gardens rich and heady with scented, casual and homely plants. Properly known as *Hesperis matronalis*, sweet rocket is a short-lived perennial, usually grown as a biennial and has white, mauve or purple flowers during early summer. Queen Marie Antoinette was fond of the lovely, scented flowers and while imprisoned during the late 1700s was taken bunches of sweet rocket, pinks and tuberoses each day. Like many other long-cultivated plants it is known by many names, including Queen's gillofers, summer lilac and rogue's gillifers.

> *The rose is red, the violet's blue*
> *The gilly-flower sweet, and so are you.*

(An Easter-day rhyme in Oxfordshire)

*Detail of*
At Madehurst, Sussex.

63

# Wallflowers

Wallflowers, defying gravity and confidently clinging to garden walls, were introduced from Europe during the Norman Conquest in the eleventh century. Known as wallstock-gillofer, gillyflower and giroflier, this fragrant flower gained fame during the fourteenth century when it flowered on the walls of a Scottish castle. The son of a border chieftain fell in love with Elizabeth, daughter of the Earl of March. Unfortunately, she was betrothed to another and met with imprisonment from her father. Her amorous admirer, disguised as a minstrel, sang songs of elopement beneath her window and she dropped a wallflower to acknowledge her agreement. Later, as she was trying to make her escape, she fell and died. Devastated by her death, her lover wandered throughout Europe as a minstrel, wearing a sprig of wallflower and singing songs of lost love.

*A detail of*
A Country Cottage Near
Whitenash.

A Country Cottage Near Whitenash, Warwickshire, 1887
*David Woodlock (1842-1929), private collection.*

The Farm Garden, Bossington
*Arthur Claude Strachan (1865-1954),*
*private collection.*

# Sweet Williams

Sweet williams are members of the carnation family, native to Europe and widely grown as biennials, being sown one year to produce plants that bear flowers during the following one. They are thought to have been introduced into Britain by Carthusian monks during the twelfth century. Popular legend suggests they were named after William the Conqueror, but it is more likely that they gained their name from St William of Aquitaine, a less aggressive gentleman and far more worthy of the appellation 'sweet'. It gathered other common names, some which were later given to other flowers. London pride was one, but currently referring to *Saxifraga* x *urbium*. Sweet williams have also been known as London tufts, cull-me-to-you (from the word to cull or coll meaning to embrace) and velvet williams.

*Detail of*
The Farm Garden, Bossington.

Crossing the Ford
*Arthur Claude Strachan (1865-1954),*
*Baron Fine Art.*

*Detail from*
Crossing the Ford.

# Mignonette

Mignonette was probably introduced from Egypt to Europe by the Romans and for centuries was valued solely for the sedative quality of its seeds. It was not until the mid-1700s that its garden and pot-plant value became appreciated. Once established, it was grown widely, though it came to be particularly associated with London. It was said that Paris streets were known for the bouquet of ground coffee, while those of London were famous for the heady, characteristic scent of mignonette. It gained popularity in country areas and was recommended in the influential magazine *The Cottage Gardener* during the mid-nineteenth century, both for growing in pots and in borders. Mignonette was a fashionable flower in much of Europe, especially in Paris. Napoleon collected seeds of mignonette during his Egyptian campaign in 1798 and gave them to the Empress Josephine, who set the style in France of growing it in pots.

*A detail from*
A Pretty Cottage Garden.

## *from* COME HITHER

*Art weary? here's the place*
*For weariness to rest,*
*These flowers are herbs of grace*
*To cure the aching breast;*
*Soft beds these mossy banks*
*Where dewdrops only weep,*
*Where Nature 'turns God thanks*
*And sings herself to sleep.*
*Art troubled with strife? come hither,*
*Here's peace and summer weather.*

*Come hither for pleasure who list –*
*Here are oak boughs for a shade:*
*These leaves they will hide from the mist*
*Ere the sun his broad disk has displayed.*
*Here is peace if thy bosom be troubled,*
*Here is rest – if thou'rt weary, sit down –*
*Here pleasure you'll find it is doubled,*
*For content is life's only crown.*
*Disciples of sorrow, come hither,*
*For no blasts my joys can wither.*

John Clare (1793-1864)

A Pretty Cottage Garden
*Alfred Glendening (fl.1861-1903),*
*Barn Gallery.*

Still Life, Apple Blossom and Lilac
*Rosa Appleton (fl.1880–1902),*
*private collection.*

# Lilac

**Summer Flowers**
*Jean Capeinick (1838–1890).*

Known to the Turks as fox's tail, the common lilac arrived in
Europe from Turkey during the sixteenth century and was
grown and acclaimed by the London barber-surgeon and botanist
John Gerard towards the end of the 1500s for its delightfully
sweet fragrance. It is native to the Balkans and it is thought that
it was collected by the Turks when they overran that area about a
century earlier. At the beginning of the 1800s there were only
blue and white forms - as well as a few minor variations - of the
common lilac. The first named variety appeared in 1832, but it
was not until the 1880s that the wealth of new ones were
introduced.

**An English Cottage Garden**
*William Stephen Coleman (1829-1904), private collection.*

At Brook Farm, Leymoor, Yorkshire
*Charles Collins (fl.1867–1903), private collection.*

# The Herb Garden

In the Garden
*Thomas Lloyd (1849–1910), private collection.*

A Study of Wildflowers and Mint
*Anonymous (c.1900).*

# Mint

Few Victorian cottage gardeners would not have cultivated a clump of spearmint with which to make mint sauce, mint jelly, mint-vinegar and other country delights such as mint cake and mint punch. More practically and fundamentally, however, many cottagers used fresh or dried mint to keep mice away from food. It was also an inexpensive way to keep teeth clean and to freshen breath. Other mints were also found in cottage gardens, including peppermint, which subsequently found fame in peppermint toothpaste.

*Here's flowers for you;*
*Hot lavender, mints, savory, marjoram;*
(William Shakespeare)

# Clary

Few cottage gardens could afford to be without clary (*Salvia sclarea*), brightening borders and creating a captivating perfume. The large leaves are surmounted in mid-summer by tubular, blue-white flowers, bringing freshness to the garden. A versatile plant, clary has many uses. In kitchens, the leaves are used fresh or dried to flavour casseroles and soups, while in ancient times clary was widely used as a medicinal herb, often to clear the sight. The name clary was gradually modified into clear eye. During the nineteenth century the leaves were used as a substitute for hops and said to 'produce an effect of insane exhilaration of spirits, followed by severe headache'.

*Mint should never be cut with iron.*
(Superstition)

Feeding the Ducks
*Henry John King (1855-1924), Julian Simon.*

Une Chaumiere et un Coeur
*Henri-Gaston Darien (1864-1926),*
*Galerie Berko.*

# Rosemary

Young Love
*Gunning King (1859-1940),*
*Roger Widdas Fine Paintings.*

Although a Mediterranean shrub, rosemary has been known in Britain since Roman times and was mentioned in herbals from the eleventh century onwards. As a multi-purpose cottage garden plant it excels, providing scented flowers and medicinal remedies. Strangely, it was both a funeral and wedding flower. Anne of Cleaves, for example, is said to have displayed it when she married Henry VIII, while the tradition of throwing sprigs of rosemary into graves endured well into the nineteenth century. Rosemary flourishes in most well-drained soils and sunny positions, but if it dies remember the adage 'Where rosemary flourishes, the mistress rules' and enquire upon a rebellious husband. Common names for rosemary include polar plant, compass-weed and compass plant. These names all refer to the fact that the plant mainly bears flowers on its southerly side and so indicates which direction is north.

*Where rosemary flourishes,*
*The mistress rules.*

(Superstiton)

Here's fine rosemary, sage and thyme,
Come buy my ground ivy.
Here's feverfew, gilliflowers and rue,
Come buy my knotted marjoram ho!
Come buy my mint, my fine green mint,
Here's lavender for your clothes,
Here's parsley and winter savoury,
And heartsease which all do choose,
Here's balm, and hissop and cinquefoil,
Let none despise and merry cries
Of famous London Town.

Here's penny royal and marygolds,
Come buy my sage of virtue O!
Come buy my wormwood and mugwort,
Here's fine herbs of every sort,
And southern wood that's very good,
Dandelion and horseleek,
Here's Dragon's tongue and horehound;
Let none despise the merry cried
Of famous London Town.

(Street Cry)

Ann Hathaway's Cottage
*Arthur Claude Strachan (1865-1954),*
*Haynes Fine Art.*

**Playing with the Kittens**
*John Lynas Gray (b.1869), private collection.*

Wild Roses
*William Stephen Coleman*
*(1829-1904), private collection.*

Learning to Walk
*Myles Birket Foster (1825-1899),*
*Polak Gallery.*

# Catmint

The earliest catmint grown in gardens is not the hybrid known today, *Nepeta x faassenii*, but rather the native *N. cataria*, which was cultivated as early as 1265 and known as nepta or kattesminte. Both plants have a curious fascination for cats, who nibble leaves, rub against plants and then roll over on them. Curiously, however, when plants are transplanted into a garden they are usually damaged by cats, but when grown from seed are left alone. This is reflected in the saying:

*If you set it, the cats will eat it,*
*If you sow it, the cats don't know it.*

Before the introduction of tea from China, the English peasantry made an infusion from catmint, which was said to be very wholesome. Conversely, rats are reputed to hate the plant and will not go near it, even when driven by hunger.

# Tansy

Tansy (*Tanacetum vulgare*) is a familiar British native, abundant in hedgerows and waste places and clearly at one time popular in gardens. In the 1800s, the poet John Clare wrote:

*... golden-rods and tansy running high*
*The o'er the pale-top smiled on passers-by;*
*Flowers in my time which every one would praise*
*Though thrown like weeds from gardens nowadays.*

In the fourteenth century, tansy was used to heal wounds, while later in country areas an infusion of tansy was used to cure fevers. More popularly, however, it was an essential part of tansy-pudding, a traditional Easter dish. It was also a country cure to keep flies from meat and to drive bugs from beds.

# Parsley

Culinary herbs, like parsley, were essential during earlier centuries to cloak the incipient decay in meat. However, many of these culinary herbs also had a medicinal value which in country areas could be invaluable. The leaves of parsley, for example, were laid on inflamed eyes to soothe them and a poultice made from bread and parsley took away bruises caused by falls. Additionally, its roots could be boiled and eaten.

*Parsley seed always goes nine times*
*to the Devil before it comes up.*
(Proverb)

# Sage

Sage (*Salvia officinalis*) has long been grown in cottage gardens and earlier in monastical enclaves, having been introduced from southern Europe by the Romans. Apart from its culinary qualities it has been credited with other virtues, including whitening teeth and strengthening gums. Sage tea was prized by the Chinese, Italian peasants ate sage leaves with bread and butter, while in England and France it was said to mitigate against grief. Indeed, at one time it was customary for it to be planted on graves. If these qualities were not enough, an Arabian proverb suggests its ability to bring long life.

*If the sagebush thrives and grows,*
*The master's not master and he knows.*
(Superstition)

Feeding the Doves
*Ernest Walbourn (fl.1897-1904), private collection.*

In the Garden
*Charles James Lewis (1830-1892), Priests Antiques.*

# Rue

A Surrey Lane
*Walter Waller Caffyn (fl.c. 1876), private collection.*

Rue, a hardy evergreen, has long been popular as a cottage garden plant. The attractive blue-green leaves, which were valued by cottagers for their medicinal and antiseptic properties, were planted in borders, giving an attractive, decorative effect. In the seventeenth and eighteenth centuries, lawcourts were strewn with rue as protection against jail-fever and rue-water when sprinkled in houses was said to kill fleas. Rue was also one of the ingredients used to make Vinegar of the Four Thieves, a tonic taken by thieves throughout Europe to ward off fever, enabling them to enter and steal from plague-ridden houses. Rue was also frequently used to form brushes for sprinkling holy water in churches, and for this reason it became known as Herb of Grace.

# Strewing Herbs

Discouraging lice and fleas in cottages was essential and many special herbs were strewn on floors to repel insects and to create a pleasing and varied scent. More than twenty different plants, including lavender, tansy, balm, basil, marjoram, sage and winter savory – all popular cottage garden plants – were used. Rushes were also employed, especially the sweet flag (*Acorus calamus*) also known as sweet sedge, which had an agreeably sweet fragrance and was often strewn in churches. It was, however, expensive, and its frequent and extravagant use as a strewing herb was a charge levied at Cardinal Wolsey by Henry VIII in 1592, when he wished to oust Wolsey from his position in order to force through his plans to divorce Catherine of Aragon.

The 1st of May, Garland Day
*Myles Birket Foster (1825-1899),*
*private collection.*

Picking Honeysuckle
*Sophie Anderson (1823-1898), private collection.*

**In the Orchard**
*Walter Boodle (fl.1891-1908), Haynes Fine Art.*

# The Fruits of the Garden

Feeding the Chickens
*Ernest Walbourn (fl.1897-1904), Hampshire Gallery.*

In the Orchard
*Edward Elliott (fl.1920-34), Haynes Fine Art.*

# Fruit Trees

Country routine was often dictated by sayings and a few referred to fruit trees. Even the best time for eating fruit was put in verse:

> *Till St. Swithin's Day be past,*
> *The apples be not fit to taste.*

Picking apples for storing was said to be best 'in the moon's dark, lest harmful rays cause them to rot'. And the proper time to graft apples trees was indicated in rhyme:

> *From moon being changed,*
> *Till past be the prime,*
> *For graffing (grafting) and cropping,*
> *Is very good time.*

## from A FAREWELL

> *Farewell, thou little nook of mountain-ground,*
> *Thou rocky corner in the lowest stair*
> *Of that magnificent temple which doth bound*
> *One side of our whole vale with grandeur rare;*
> *Sweet garden-orchard, eminently fair,*
> *The loveliest spot that man hath ever found,*
> *Farewell! — we leave thee to heaven's peaceful care,*
> *Thee, and the cottage which thou dost surround.*

William Wordsworth (1770-1850)

## LOVELIEST OF TREES

*Loveliest of trees, the cherry now*
*Is hung with bloom along the bough,*
*And stands about the woodland ride*
*Wearing white for Eastertide.*

*Now, of my threescore years and ten,*
*Twenty will not come again,*
*And take from seventy springs a score,*
*It only leaves me fifty more.*

*And since to look at things in bloom*
*Fifty springs are little room,*
*About the woodlands I will go*
*To see the cherry hung with snow.*

A.E. Houseman (1859-1936)

Apple Blossom
*Anne Jenkins (fl.1876-1885),*
*Bill Minns.*

Picking Buttercups
*Helen Allingham (1848-1926), Bourne Gallery.*

# Wassailing Orchards

Protecting fruit trees from evil and bringing them good luck was, for a long time, part of the Christmas festivities. It was sometimes performed on Christmas Day or New Year's Day, but most often on Twelfth Night. Villagers would collect around the largest tree and pour cider over its roots. Sometimes the lowest branches were lowered and dipped in a pale of cider, and a piece of toast or cake soaked in the brew put in the fork of a branch. Villagers would toast the tree and then sing to it:

> *Here's to thee, old apple tree,*
> *Whence though may'st bud, and whence though*
> *        may'st blow,*
> *And whence though may'st bear apples enow.*
> *Hatsfull, capsfull, bushel-bushel sacksfull,*
> *And my pockets full too!*
> *                        Hurrah!*

## *from* TO AUTUMN

*Season of mists and mellow fruitfulness,*
*Close bosom-friend of the maturing sun;*
*Conspiring with him how to load and bless*
*With fruit the vines that round the thatch-eves run;*
*To bend with apples the moss'd cottage trees,*
*And fill all fruit with ripeness to the core;*
*To swell the gourd, and plump the hazel shells*
*With a sweet kernel; to set budding more,*
*And still more, later flowers for the bees,*
*Until they think warm days will never cease,*
*For Summer has o'er-brimm'd their clammy cells.*

John Keats (1795-1821)

Daughters of Eve
*Sir Frank Dicksee (1853-1928).*

## HARVESTING RHYMES

*September blow soft,*
*Till the fruits in the loft.*

*A cherry year, A merry year;*
*A pear year, A dear year;*
*A plum year, A dumb year.*

*Till St. Swithin's Day be past,*
*The apples be not fit to taste.*

## *from* THE ORCHARD AND THE HEATH

*I chanced upon an early walk to spy*
*A troop of children through an orchard gate:*
    *The boughs hung low, the grass was high;*
    *They had but to lift hands or wait*
*For fruits to fill them; fruits were all their sky.*

*They shouted, running on from tree to tree,*
*And played the game the wind plays, on and round.*
    *'Twas visible invisible glee*
    *Pursuing; and a fountain's sound*
*Of laughter spouted, pattering fresh on me.*

*I could have watched them till the daylight fled,*
*Their pretty bower made such a light of day.*
    *A small one tumbling sang, 'Oh! head!'*
    *The rest to comfort her straightway*
*Seized on a branch and thumped down apples red.*

George Meredith (1828-1909)

In the Apple Orchard
*William Affleck (1868-1943), Haynes Fine Art.*

Beehives in a Flower Garden
*R.T. Wilding (fl.1895-1915), Catto Gallery.*

A Summer Afternoon
*Frank Walton (1840-1928),*
*Anthony Mitchell Fine Paintings.*

## *from* CHIMES

I

*Honey-flowers to the honey-comb*
*And the honey-bee's from home.*

*A honey-comb and a honey-flower,*
*And the bee shall have his hour.*

*A honeyed heart for the honey-comb,*
*And the humming bee flies home*

*A heavy heart in the honey-flower*
*And the bee has had his hour*

II

*A honey-cell's in the honeysuckle,*
*and the honey-bee knows it well.*

*The honey-comb has a heart of honey,*
*and the humming bee's so bonny.*

*A honey-flower's the honeysuckle,*
*And the bee's in the honey-bell.*

*The honeysuckle is sucked of honey,*
*And the bee is heavy and bonny*

Dante Gabriel Rossetti (1828-1882).

# Bees

Happy, contented bees were vital in country communities and until the late 1800s it was thought that the family's fortunes were closely associated with those of their bees. Indeed, the bond between bees and owner was so strong that many countrymen claimed to recognise their own bees. Countryfolk often told their bees about forthcoming marriages and it was traditional for white ribbons to be tied around hives on wedding days. If a swarm of bees appeared on a wedding day it was thought a happy omen. In the same way, if a death occurred in the family it was customary to tell the bees and, in the late eighteenth century, the hives were turned at the moment that the deceased was taken out of the house.

*If the bees stay at home,*
*Rain will soon come;*
*If they fly away,*
*Fine will be the day.*

(Weather lore)

*A swarm of bees in May,*
*Is worth a load of hay.*
*A swarm of bees in June,*
*Is worth a silver spoon.*
*A swarm of bees in July,*
*Is not worth a fly.*

(Bee rhymes)

In the Cottage Garden, Alveston
*Arthur Claude Strachan (1865-1954),*
*Galerie George.*

## WHERE THE BEE SUCKS

*Where the bee sucks, there suck I:*
*In a cowslips's bell I lie;*
*There I couch when owls do cry.*
*On the bat's back I do fly*
*After summer merrily:*
*Merrily, merrily, shall I live now,*
*Under the blossom that hangs on the bough.*

William Shakespeare (1564-1616)

A Spring Hedgerow with Pansies
*George Goodman (fl.c. 1860-1868),*
*private collection.*

Picking Fruit
in a Suffolk
Garden
*L.L. Pocock
(1850-1919),
Bourne Gallery.*

# Balm

Common balm (*Melissa officinalis*) is a versatile herb. As well as brightening cottage gardens with its flowers, it played an important part in keeping bees. Its leaves were rubbed on the insides of skeps to help keep bees together and encourage others to join them. Its scent was also said to guide bees home. Indeed, the old Greek name for balm, Melissophyllon, means beloved by bees. Keeping bees happy and contented was important for nineteenth-century cottage gardeners for sugar was scare and expensive and honey and wax were vital to the economy.

# Mead

Skeps of bees were essential to the production of mead, which was created from honey and water and fermented with yeast. Mead was known to the Ancient Greeks, spreading to England and by 1665 more than fifty recipes were known. A variation known as sack mead included the addition of sack and brandy. Sack was strong white wine imported from Spain and the Canaries into England during the sixteenth and seventeenth centuries. Up to Victorian times mead was drunk by all classes, after which it remained the drink of villagers. Some meads had cowslips, cloves, nutmeg or ginger added to them.

A Cottage Garden
*Ernest Walbourn (fl.1897-1904),*
*private collection.*

*Onion skin,*
*Very thin,*
*Mild weather coming in;*
*Onion skin thick and tough,*
*Coming winter cold and rough.*

(Fortelling of bad weather)

A Garden at Warwick
*George Hodgson (1847-1921),*
*Anthony Mitchell Fine Paintings.*

# Cabbages

Long a staple part of the cottagers diet, cabbages were grown in most cottage gardens. It is probable that they were introduced into Britain by the Romans, who greatly valued them. Leeks were also prized in ancient Rome; Nero subsisted on them while training his voice! Later, cabbages were often listed as worts, but by the late 1600s were prominent vegetables, with detailed instructions on their cultivation.

*He would canter nine miles around a cabbage.*
(Proverb - Said of a verbose person)

Feeding the Doves
*Ernest Walbourn (fl.1897-1904), Fine Art of Oakham.*

# Geese and Hens

**M**ost cottage gardeners would keep a small number of chickens, leaving them to wander freely in gardens, scratching the ground for food. Keeping hens, however, was often full of taboos. Even until the late nineteenth century it was thought unlucky to start a hen on a Sunday or to hatch eggs during May, and it was believed that only an odd number of eggs should be used. Among other superstitions was the belief that if less than thirteen primroses were taken indoors in spring as a posy, each hen would only hatch that number of eggs. Carrying fertile hen's eggs over running water was also unwise.

*Whistling maid and crowing hen, is neither good for God nor men.*

(Proverb)

Feeding the Chickens
*Henry Towneley Green (1836-1899),*
*Manchester International Fine Art.*

Spring in the Orchard
*Alfred William Parsons (1847-1920),*
*Bourne Gallery.*

Feeding the Hens
*Joseph Kirkpatrick (fl.1890–1928), Roger Widdas Fine Paintings.*

Tending the Garden
*Jean Beauduin (1851-1916), Haynes Fine Art.*

# *Vegetables*

For centuries, the vegetable garden was fundamental to cottagers, providing them with the staples of their diet. By the early 1800s, the main vegetables grown in cottage gardens were potatoes, runner beans, broad beans, peas, leeks, onions and cabbages. Salad plants and herbs were also important. Potatoes and beans were especially useful and were sometimes used to help feed pigs, another important cottage commodity. Competition developed between cottagers to grow the best - or biggest - vegetable and this led to annual horticultural exhibitions.

*Potatoes and apples*
*And peas, the fat marrow,*
*Dame Durgin can sell you,*
*From her well-stored barrow.*

(Street Cry)

Peeling Vegetables
*Fanny Fildes (d.1927),*
*Gavin Graham Gallery.*

*When the elm leaf is as big as a mouse's ear,*
*Then to sow barley, never fear.*

*When the elum leaves are as big as a farden,*
*'Tis time to plant kidney beans in the garden.*

(Sowing rhymes)

Tending the Garden
*Jennie Greaves Dewey,*
*private collection.*

Buy ripe Strawberries, fine Strawberries
Ripe Strawberries, ripe Strawberries, O!
In lovely beds, by nature taught,
The Strawberries are displayed,
And hence for use, to market brought,
By this industrious maid.

Here strawberries, the best,
Nice Hautboys fresh and fine;
With cream by all confest,
Delicious vespertine.

(Street Cry)

The Bullfinch
*Marcus Stone (1840-1921),*
*Apollo Gallery.*

Wild Strawberries and a Butterfly
*Albert Lucas (1828-1918),*
*Beaton Brown Fine Paintings.*

# Soft Fruits

Still Life, Roses and Fruit
*Joseph Robinson (fl.1862-1874),*
*Cooper Fine Arts.*

The vitality and imagination that abounded in the Victorian age also revealed itself in the range of fruits that were widely grown. Hedgerow fruits had always been popular, while strawberries could be easily increased by severing rooted runners. This succulent fruit was cultivated in its wild, sweet-tasting form in Elizabethan times but in the early 1800s a Chilean species yielding large, red fruits grew in popularity. Gooseberries, so named because a sauce made from the berries had been traditionally served with roast goose, were popular in Victorian cottage gardens. The tradition of holding an annual competition to find the largest berry grew up in certain areas, particularly the north of England. One trick to ensure success was to feed the plant with a sugar solution through a wick inserted in the stalk. Berries that did not make it to the prize table were used to make jam and for stewing. They were also eaten fresh and were acclaimed as refreshing. Red and white currants, as well as raspberries, were also popular.

Daydreaming
*Dewey Bates (1851-1899), Anthony Mitchell Fine Paintings.*

# The Language of Flowers

Primroses
*William Hough (fl.1850-1900), Philip Gale.*

*Still Life, Pansies and Pelargoniums*
*Thomas Collier (fl.1850-1874),*
*private collection.*

The fashion for using flowers to express emotions reached its height in Europe in the nineteenth century, when the significance of each flower and the way in which it was presented were widely known, and even the smallest of posies was chosen with great care, to convey the correct meaning. This language of flowers was, however, already well established and had been introduced into western Europe in the eighteenth century.

In 1716 the celebrated letter-writer and poet Lady Mary Wortley Montagu accompanied her husband on a trip to Constantinople – modern day Istanbul – where she learned of the Turkish custom for lovers use flowers to convey messages. During her stay, she sent a Turkish love letter to England which interpreted the meaning of some plants, flowers and spices. The wonder of flowers, she proposed, was that words and messages of love could be passed in a refined and subtle manner without *'inking the fingers'*. On her return to England she brought additional information about the language of flowers.

The passing of messages via the floral code was then taken up by the French, only to return later to England during the reign of Queen Victoria through Madame de la Tour's book *Le Langage de Fleurs*. Many of the phrases contained in this book, however, were risqué and too lusty for gentile Victorian society. The language in English books on the subject published at that time was, therefore, toned down.

More than 800 flowers have special meanings associated with them. Indeed, there are over 30 for roses alone. Messages can become quite complex when several flowers are presented in a bouquet. The way in which flowers were worn and presented had a meaning in addition to the sentiments attached to individual flowers. A flower bent towards the right would signify *I*, while one extending to the left would mean *you*. A red rosebud leaning to the left would say: *You are pure and lovely*. Foliage had an additional significance, leaves meaning hope, thorns danger. Therefore, a rose with the thorns plucked off but the leaves left intact would convey *hopeful love and confidence*.

The language is further enriched by the hand – left or right – that proffers the flowers, as well the one that receives it. An affirmative is suggested by the right hand, while the left one indicates a negative. Thus a provence rose offered by the right hand underlines the sentiment *My heart is in flames* and, if received by a right hand, would give satisfaction to the giver.

If flowers could not be presented personally they were sent in boxes tied with ribbons, and these too held a message, depending on where the knot was tied.

## A

A beauty *Orchis*
A belle *Orchis*
A smile *Sweet william*
A token *Ox-eye daisy, laurestina*
Absence *Wormwood*
Abuse not *Crocus*
Acknowledgement *Canterbury bell*
Activity *Thyme*
Adversity, energy in *Camomile*
Admiration *Amethyst*
Adoration *Dwarf sunflower*
Adresses rejected *Ice plant*
Advice *Rhubarb*
Affectation *Morning glory*
Affection *Mossy saxifrage, pear, sorrel*
Affection, bonds of *Gillyflower*
Affection, enduring *Gorse*
Afterthought *Michaelmas Daisy*
Age *Guelder rose*
Agreement *Straw*
Alas! for my poor heart *Deep red carnation*
Always lovely *Indian double pink*
Am I forgotten? *Holly*
Ambition *Mountain laurel*
Amiability *Jasmine*
Anticipation *Gooseberry*
Anxiety, tranquillise my *Christmas rose*
Anxious and trembling *Red columbine*
Appointed meeting *Everlasting pea*
Ardour *Cuckoo plant, arum lily*
Argument *Fig*
Artifice *Acanthus*
Assiduous to please *Sprig of ivy with tendrils*
Assignation *Pimpernel*
Attachment *Indian jasmine*
Austerity *Common thistle*

Still Life, Roses and Summer Flowers
*Maria Harrison (fl.1850),*
*Thompson's Gallery.*

Avarice *Scarlet auricula*
Aversion *Indian single pink*

## B

Bantering *Southernwood*
Bashful shame *Deep red rose*
Bashfulness *Peony*
Be mine *Four-leaved clover*
Beautiful, call me not *Unique rose*
Beautiful eyes *Variegated tulip*
Beauty *Parti-coloured daisy, full red rose*
Beauty, a *Orchis*

Beauty always new *China rose*
Beauty and prosperity *Red-leaved rose*
Beauty, capricious *Lady's slipper, musk rose*
Beauty, delicate *Hibiscus*
Beauty, divine *American cowslip*
Beauty, lasting *Stock*
Beauty, mental *Clematis*
Beauty, pensive *Laburnum*
Beauty, rustic *French honeysuckle*
Beauty, unconscious *Burgundy rose*
Beauty, unfading *Gillyflower*
Belief *Passion-flower*
Belle, a *Orchis*
Benevolence *Potato*
Betrayal *Judas tree*
Beware *Oleander*
Beware of excess *Saffron*
Blackness *Ebony*
Bluntness *Borage*
Blushes *Marjoram*
Boaster, a *Hydrangea*
Boldness *Pink*
Bonds *Convolvulus*
Bonds of affection *Gillyflower*
Bravery *Oak leaves*
Bulk *Water melon, gourd*
Bury me amid Nature's beauties *Persimon*

## C

Call me not beautiful *Unique rose*
Change *Pimpernel*
Changeable disposition *Rye grass*
Charity *Turnip*
Charming *Cluster of musk roses*
Cheerfulness in old age *American Starwort*
Cheerfulness under adversity *Chrysanthemum*
Childishness *Buttercup*

Chivalry *Great yellow daffodil*
Cleanliness *Hyssop*
Coldheartedness *Lettuce*
Colour of my life *Coral honeysuckle*
Come down *Jacob's ladder*
Comforting *Scarlet geranium*
Compassion *Allspice*
Concealed love *Motherwort*
Concealed merit *Coriander*
Confidence *Lilac polyanthus*
Conjugal love *Lime*
Consolation *Red poppy*
Cordiality *Peppermint*
Counterfeit *Mock orange*
Crime *Tamarisk*
Criticism *Cucumber*
Cure *Balm of gilead*
Cure for heartache *Cranberry, swallow-wort*
Curiosity *Sycamore*

**D**

Danger *Rhododendron, monkshood*
Dangerous pleasures *Tuberose*
Dauntlessness *Sea lavender*
Death *Cypress*
Deceit *Flytrap, dogsbane*
Deceitful charms *Thorn-apple*
Deception *White cherry*
Decrease of love *Yellow sweet-brier, yellow rose*
Dejection *Lichen*
Delay *Eupatorium*
Delicacy *Cornflower*
Departure *Sweet pea*
Despair *Cypress and marigold*
Devotion *Heliotrope*
Difficulties, I surmount *Mistletoe*

Lilies
*Sidney Percy Kendrick (d. 1955),*
*Haynes Fine Art.*

Dignity *Cloves, laurel-leaved magnolia*
Disappointment *Carolina syringa*
Discretion *Lemon blossoms, maidenhair*
Disdain *Yellow carnation, rue*
Distinction *Cardinal flower*
Distrust *Lavender*
Do me justice *Sweet chestnut tree*
Do not abuse *Saffron*
Domestic industry *Flax*

**E**

Early attachment *Thornless rose*
Early friendship *Blue periwinkle*

Early youth *Primrose*
Education *Cherry tree*
Elegance and grace *Yellow jasmine*
Elegance, mature *Pomegranate flower*
Elevation *Scotch fir*
Enchantment *Holly herb*
Enduring affection *Gorse*
Energy in adversity *Camomile*
Envy *Crane's bill, bramble*
Esteem *Garden sage*
Esteem and love *Strawberry tree*
Esteem but not love *Spiderwort*
Evanescent pleasure *Poppy*
Excellence, perfect *Strawberry*
Excellence, unpretending *Camellia japonica*
Excess, beware of *Saffron*
Expectation *Anemone*
Expected meeting *Nutmeg, geraniums*
Extent *Gourd*
Extinguished hopes *Major convolvulus*
Extravagance, fantastic *Scarlet poppy*

**F**

Faithfulness *Blue violet, heliotrope*
Falsehood *Yellow lily*
Fame *Tulip*
Fantastic extravagance *Scarlet poppy*
Farewell *Michaelmas daisy*
Fascination *Carnation, honesty*
Fashion *Lady's mantle*
Fate *Hemp*
Feasting *Parsley*
Fecundity *Hollyhock*
Female ambition *White hollyhock*
Female fidelity *Speedwell*
Festivity *Parsley*
Fickleness *Pink larkspur*

Fidelity in love *Lemon blossoms*
Filial love *Virgin's bower*
Finesse *Sweet william*
Fire *Fleur-de-luce*
First emotions of love *Purple lilac*
Fitness *Sweet flag*
Flame *Fleur-de-lis, iris*
Flee away *Pennyroyal*
Folly *Columbine*
Foolishness *Pomegranate*
Foresight *Holly*
Forget me not *Forget-me-not*
Fraternal love *Woodbine*
Freedom *Water willow*
Freshness *Damask rose*
Friends, thoughts of absent *Zinnia*
Friendship *Rose acacia*

## G

Gaiety *Butterfly orchis, yellow lily*
Gain *Cabbage*
Gallantry *A nosegay, sweet william*
Generosity *Orange tree*
Generous and devoted affection *French honeysuckle*
Genius *Plane tree*
Gentility *Geranium, pompon rose*
Girlhood *White rosebud*
Gladness *Myrrh*
Gladness, youthful *Spring crocus*
Glory *Bay tree, laurel*
Good wishes *Sweet basil*
Goodness *Mercury*
Grace *Multiflora rose*
Grace and elegance *Yellow jasmine*
Gracefulness *Birch tree*
Grandeur *Ash tree*
Grief *Harebell, marigold*

A Posy of Pretty Flowers
*Carl Bauerle (1831-1912),*
*Haynes Fine Art.*

## H

Happy love *Bridal rose*
Hatred *Basil*
Haughtiness *Purple larkspur, tall sunflower*
Health *Iceland moss*
Heart's mystery, the *Crimson polyanthus*
Heartlessness *Hydrangea*
Hidden worth *Coriander*
Honesty *Honesty*
Hope *Flowering almond, hawthorn, snowdrop*
Hope extinguished *Major convolvulus*
Hope in adversity *Spruce pine*
Hopeless love *Yellow tulip*
Hopeless, not heartless *Love-lies-bleeding*
Hospitality *Oak tree*
Humility *Broom, small bindweed, field lilac*

## I

I am too happy *Cape jasmine*
I am worthy of you *White rose*
I am your captive *Peach blossom*
I aspire to your smile *Daily rose*
I attach myself to you *Indian jasmine*
I change but in death *Bay leaf*
I declare against you *Liquorice*
I desire a return of affection *Jonquil*
I die if neglected *Laurestina*
I engage you for the next dance *Ivy geranium*
I feel your kindness *Flax*
I have a message for you *Iris*
I live for thee *Cedar leaf*
I love *Red chrysanthemum*
I surmount difficulties *Mistletoe*
I will not answer hastily *Monthly honeysuckle*
I will not survive you *Black mulberry*
Imagination *Lupin*
Immortality *Amaranth*
Impatience *Yellow balsam*
Impatient resolves *Red balsam*
Inconstancy *Evening primrose*
Inconstancy in love *Wild honeysuckle*
Incorruptible *Cedar of lebanon*
Independence *Wild plum tree, white oak*
Indifference *Candytuft, mustard seed*
Indiscretion *Almond tree*
Ingenuity *Pencil-leaved geranium*
Ingratitude *Buttercup, wild ranunculus*
Injustice *Hop*
Innocence *White daisy, white violet*
Innocence, youthful *White lilac*
Insincerity *Foxglove*
Insinuation *Great bindweed*
Inspiration *Angelica*
Instability *Dahlia*
Ireland *Shamrock*

## J

Jealousy *French marigold, yellow rose*
Jest *Southernwood*
Joy *Wood sorrel*
Joys to come *Celandine*
Justice, do me *Sweet chestnut tree*
Justice, shall be done to you *Coltsfoot*

## K

Keep your promises *Plum tree*
Knowledge, useful *Parsley*

## L

Lamentation *Aspen tree*
Lasting pleasure *Everlasting pea*
Levity *Larkspur*
Life *Lucerne*
Lightheartedness *Shamrock*
Lightness *Larkspur*
Longevity *Fig*
Love *Blue violet, myrtle, rose*
Love in idleness *Wild violet*
Love is dangerous *Carolina rose*
Love of nature *Magnolia*
Love returned *Ambrosia*
Love's oracle *Dandelion*
Love ardent *Balsam*
Love, chaste *Acacia*
Love, confession of *Moss rosebud*
Love, declaration of *Red tulip*
Love, estranged *Lotus flower*
Love, forsaken *Creeping willow*
Love, only deserve my *Campion rose*
Love, platonic *Rose acacia*
Love, pure and ardent *Double red pink*

Beautiful Summer Flowers
*Alexandre Debrus, Galerie Berko.*

Love, secret *Toothwort, yellow acacia*
Love, slighted *Yellow chrysanthemum*
Love, sweet and secret *Honey flower*
Love, the first emotions of *Purple lilac*
Lovely, thou art all that is *Austrian rose*
Love, true *Forget-me-not*
Lowliness *Bramble*

## M

Majesty *Crown imperial, imperial lily*
Malevolence *Lobelia*
Marriage *Ivy*
Maternal affection *Cinquefoil*
Maternal love *Moss*
Maternal tenderness *Wood sorrel*
Mature elegance *Pomegranate flower*
Meekness *Birch*
Meeting, an appointed *Everlasting pea*

Meeting, an expected *Nutmeg, geranium*
Melancholy *Dark geranium, cypress*
Memory, pleasures of *White periwinkle*
Merit, concealed *Coriander*
Merit, reward of *Bay wreath*
Message *Iris*
Modesty *White violet, white lilac*
Modesty and purity *White lily*
Mourning *Weeping willow, cypress*
Music *Oats, reeds*
My best days are past *Meadow saffron*
My compliments *Iris*
My heart is in flames *Provence rose*

## N

Nature, love of *Magnolia*
Neatness *Broom*
Night *Minor convolvulus*

## O

Old age *Tree of life*
Ornament *Hornbeam tree*

## P

Painting *Auricula*
Parental affection *Sorrel*
Passion *White dittany, yellow iris*
Patience *Dock, ox eye*
Patriotism *Nasturtium*
Peace *Olive branch*
Pensiveness *Cowslip*
Perfected loveliness *White camelia japonica*
Perform your promise *Plum tree*
Perplexity *Love-in-a-mist*
Perseverance *Canary grass, swamp magnolia*

A Bird's Nest with Hawthorn and Pink Blossom
*Charles Thomas Bale (fl.1866-1875), Hinson Fine Paintings.*

Piety, steadfast *Wild geranium*
Pity *Pine*
Play *Hyacinth*
Pleasant recollections *White periwinkle*
Pleasure and pain *Dog rose*
Poetry *Eglantine*
Poverty *Evergreen clematis*
Power *Cress*
Precaution *Golden rod*
Precocity *May rose*
Prediction *Prophetic marigold*
Presumption *Snapdragon*
Pretension *Spiked willow herb*
Prettiness *Pompon rose*
Pride *Amaryllis*
Promptness *Ten-week stock*
Prosperity *Beech tree, wheat*
Prudence *Mountain ash*

Pure and lovely *Red rosebud*
Pure love *Single red pink*
Purity *White lilac*
Purity and sweetness *White lily*

**R**

Recall *Silver-leaved geranium*
Reconciliation *Filbert, hazel*
Refusal *Striped carnation, variegated pink*
Regard *Daffodil*
Religious superstition *Aloe, passion-flower*
Remembrance *Rosemary, Forget-me-not*
Remorse *Bramble, raspberry*
Rendezvous *Chickweed*
Reserve *Maple*
Resolution *Purple columbine*
Restoration *Persicaria*

Retaliation *Scotch thistle*
Return of happiness *Lily of the valley*
Revenge *Birdsfoot trefoil*
Reverie *Flowering fen*
Reward of merit *Bay wreath*
Reward of virtue *Garland of roses*
Riches *Corn*
Rivalry *Rocket*
Rupture of a contract *Broken straw*
Rural Happiness *Yellow violet*
Rustic oracle *Dandelion*

**S**

Sadness *Dead leaves, yew*
Safety *Traveller's joy*
Satire *Prickly pear*
Self-esteem *Poet's narcissus*
Sensitiveness *Mimosa*
Sensuality *Spanish jasmine*
Sentiment, warmth of *Spearmint*
Separation *Carolina jasmine*
Severity *Branch of thorns*
Shame *Peony*
Sharpness *Barberry*
Shyness *Vetch*
Sickness *Anemone, zephyr flower*
Silence *Belladonna (deadly nightshade)*
Silliness *Fool's parsley*
Simplicity *American sweet-brier*
Sincerity *Fern, honesty*
Slander *Stinging nettle*
Sleep *White poppy*
Slighted love *Yellow chrysanthemum*
Splendid beauty *Amarylis*
Steadfast piety *Wild geranium*
Stoicism *Box tree*
Strength *Cedar, fennel*

Surprise *Truffle*
Susceptibility *Passion-flower*
Suspicion *Mushroom*
Sympathy *Balm, thrift*

**T**

Talent *White pink*
Taste *Scarlet fuchsia*
Tears *Helenium*
Temperance *Azalea*
Temptation *Apple, quince*
Thoughts *Pansy*
Thoughts of absent friends *Zinnia*
Thy frown will kill me *Currant*
Ties *Tendrils of climbing plants*
Time *White poplar*
Timidity *Amaryllis*
Tranquillise my anxiety *Christmas rose*
Tranquillity *Stonecrop*
Transient impressions *Whithered white rose*
Transport of joy *Cape jasmine*
True friendship *Oak-leaved geranium*
Truth *White chrysanthemum*

**U**

Unanimity *Phlox*
Unbelief *Judas tree*
Uncertainty *Convolvulus*
Unchangeable *Globe amaranth*
Unconscious *Red daisy*
Unexpected meeting *Lemon geranium*

The Rose Bush, *C. Lovmand (1803-1872),
Christopher Cole Fine Paintings.*

Unity *White and red rose together*
Uselessness *Meadowsweet*

**V**

Variety *Aster, mundi rose*
Victory *Palm*
Virtue *Mint*
Virtue, domestic *Sage*
Virtue, reward of *Garland of roses*
Voraciousness *Lupin*
Vulgar-minded *African marigold*

**W**

War *York rose*
Warmth of sentiment *Spearmint*
Watchfulness *Dame violet*
Widowhood *Sweet scabious*
Win me and wear me *Lady's slipper*
Winning grace *Cowslip*
Winter *Guelder rose*
Wisdom *White mulberry*
Wish, a *Foxglove*
Wit *Ragged robin*
Witchcraft *Nightshade*
Woman's love *Carnation, carnation pink*
Worth beyond beauty *Sweet alyssum*

**Y**

You are perfect *Pine apple*
You are radiant with charms *Ranunculus*
You are young and beautiful *Red rosebud*
You occupy my thoughts *Pansy, purple violet*
You please all *Branch of currants*
You will be my death *Hemlock*
Your looks freeze me *Ice plant*
Your presence revives me *Rosemary*
Your purity equals your loveliness *Orange
  blossoms*
Your qualities, like your charms are
unequalled *Peach*
Youth, early *Primrose*

**Z**

Zealousness *Elder*
Zest *Lemon*